Papermill

The American Poetry Recovery Series

Series Editor
Cary Nelson

Board of Advisors
Daniel Aaron
Houston A. Baker Jr.
Carolyn Forché
Karen Ford
Reginald Gibbons
Walter Kalaidjian
Paul Lauter
Philip Levine
Alan Wald

A list of books in the series appears at the end of this book.

Papermill

POEMS, 1927–35

Joseph Kalar

Edited by Ted Genoways

University of Illinois Press
Urbana and Chicago

Library of Congress Cataloging-in-Publication Data
Kalar, Joseph A. (Joseph Antony), 1906–1972.
Papermill: poems, 1927–35 / Joseph Kalar; edited by Ted Genoways.
p. cm. — (The American poetry recovery series)
Includes bibliographical references.
ISBN-13: 978-0-252-02949-3 (cloth : alk. paper)
ISBN-10: 0-252-02949-6 (cloth : alk. paper)
ISBN-13: 978-0-252-07200-0 (pbk. : alk. paper)
ISBN-10: 0-252-07200-6 (pbk. : alk. paper)
1. Protest poetry, American.
2. Working class—Poetry.
I. Genoways, Ted.
II. Title.
III. Series.
PS3521.A28A6   2006
811'.52—dc22   2005035213

Contents

Papermill

Introduction

Proletarian Night: The Life and Work of Joseph Kalar

TED GENOWAYS

Joseph Kalar never published a book of poems. In fact, anyone who knows the name probably knows him for one poem. A lean, well-honed labor lyric, Kalar's "Papermill" has a deserved reputation as one of the finest protest poems of the Depression era. It is a political poem, but what makes it enduring is Kalar's fierce allegiance to specificity over stock symbolism and the crafted, tightly wound rhythms that propel each line.

Described by Cary Nelson as an "almost expressionistic portrait of an abandoned factory,"[1] the poem portrays the papermill that was once the lifeblood of International Falls, Minnesota, the small working village where Kalar grew up. Now, the poem reveals, the mill has been shut down, but the workers still pace outside the iron gates in disbelief:

> Not to be believed, this dry fall
> Of unseen fog drying the oil
> And emptying the jiggling greasecups;
> Not to be believed, this unseen hand
> Weaving a filmy rust of spiderwebs
> Over these turbines and grinding gears,
> These snarling chippers and pounding jordans;
> These fingers placed to lips saying shshsh:
> Keep silent, keep silent, keep silent . . .

Since its original publication in the Leftist magazine *The Front* in 1931, "Papermill" has been reprinted numerous times—in Alfred Kreymborg's *Anthology of American Poetry*, Jack Salzman's *Social Poetry of the 1930s*, the *Heath Anthology of American Literature*, the Library of America's two-volume *American Poetry: The Twentieth Century*, and the *Oxford Anthology of Modern American Poetry*, to name but a few appearances. In his book *The Enjoyment of Poetry*, Max Eastman declared the poem "the rarest jewel so far produced by the ferment in America called proletarian poetry—and it is pure art." He explained:

> Not one suggestion what to do or how to do it, not one thought or practical meaning accurately so-called, not one hint toward the "organization of class feeling" is contained in this verse. There is not a factory boss in America possessed of sense organs and a feeling heart who could not read it with vital participation. Like [Diego] Rivera's painting it might be well admired and paid for by the Rockefellers. This is a simple matter of fact.[2]

Indeed, "Papermill" became so revered that Kalar worried it overshadowed the rest of his work. He told his close confidant Warren Huddlestone that he considered the poem "about as perfect in its way as a poem on that subject could be," but he lamented that it had been "so anthologized that I'm sick of it and almost afraid of its present grandeur pumped into it by well-meaning but slightly addled comrades."[3]

Kalar's relative obscurity is not, however, the result of the quality of his other work; it was an obscurity he *chose*. He chose to publish only in Socialist and labor magazines; because of self-doubt and overwork, he chose never to gather his poems into a collection; and, when he was not yet thirty years old, he became disenchanted by the meager effect of his poems and chose to quit writing permanently. Perhaps the decision to choose obscurity was easier for Kalar than for most writers, because writing poems was no mere artistic—and therefore egocentric—exercise for him. Though his work bears the unmistakable stamp of his wide and varied reading, he wrote poems for practical purposes; and, unlike many of his poet-activist contemporaries, he wrote about social injustices he witnessed first-hand as a worker in the isolated mills along Minnesota's border with Canada.

By the time Kalar began to second-guess his choices, his moment had passed. As Robert Shulman recently stated in *The Power of Political Art: The 1930s Literary Left Reconsidered,* "In the 1950s, when the movement was either stigmatized or ignored, the value of each individual writer was also diminished, in many cases to the point of invisibility."[4] The arrival of the 1960s brought new social causes to document and debate. However, as evidenced by the flowering of critical interest in Kalar's work in the last decade, his poems continue to resonate, and a collection of his finest poems and sketches is long overdue.

Joseph Kalar was born April 4, 1906, in Merritt, Minnesota, the second son in a family that would eventually include nine boys and a girl (who died in infancy). His parents were poor Slovenian immigrants who met and married in Cleveland. Their "bohunk name," as Kalar called it, was originally pronounced "collar," but

way before this swine first began to stir in my mother's guts the name was Anglicized out of all resemblance to the original. We now pronounce it and are that way known—Kaler, to rhyme with tailor. In other words

Jo Kalar, Jo Kalar,
His cock is a whaler,
His balls weigh 45 lbs. etc.[5]

Soon after marrying, Kalar's parents moved to northern Minnesota. Joe's father found work in one of the eight iron mines that surrounded Eveleth, and his mother picked up extra money as a barmaid in the saloon. Because Eveleth was nearly thirteen miles away from the mine, they lived in a tiny tarpaper shack in a mining village one mile east of what is now Biwabik. The village was officially called Merritt, but everyone knew it as Chicken Town because most of the families there kept chickens for eggs and meat. The creek that ran through town was grossly polluted, and rats were rampant and were "slaughtered by the hundreds." Worst of all, however, was the mine itself; in his sketch "Dust of Iron Ore," Kalar remembered, "The mine was like some horrible monster hidden in the red bowels of the earth, exhaling a poisonous vapor of dust which dropped like an unseen fog over Merritt and the little locations where the miners lived. We knew, dimly, that Merritt belonged to this monster. . . ." To escape the monster, Kalar's father moved the family in 1914 to International Falls, where he took a job in the local papermill.

That mill was the latest extension of the empire of lumber baron Edward W. Backus, president of the Minneapolis-based Backus-Brooks Company. Between 1905 and 1910, Backus expanded his business from tree farming to pulping by building first a hydroelectric dam on the Rainy River, followed by one of the world's largest sulphite mills—the mill where Kalar's father went to work, in International Falls. It was a ragtag community in those days, booming during the summer months when lumberjacks were working in the surrounding woods and sawmills, blowing their wages in town on prostitutes and gin shacks, but grim during the winter when temperatures plummeted—often to more than forty below—and the papermill kicked into full swing processing the summer harvest.[6]

The remote location and months of being cooped up by the cold made young Joe into a quiet child. He joined the Lone Scouts (a division of the Boy Scouts for boys in isolated places) and began corresponding avidly with other Lone Scouts around the world. Around the same time, he starting making regular trips to the local library, where he read adventure stories by the likes of Ernest Thompson Seton. Inspired by these tales, he began writing his own stories and published some of his earliest work in *American Scout* and *Every Boy's Journal*. He later lamented that his experience was so isolated from the Communist upheavals of the world: "The October Revolution was not a reality to me. All that I can remember, and that dimly, is a series of cartoons in the abominable *Review of Reviews* picturing a horrible bearded monster with bared wolfish teeth, booted feet trampling women and children, but even these cartoons made no impression on me, so was I in the mystical ecstacies of a boy of eleven."[7]

In high school, however, he began to become aware of revolutionary ideas through the great Scandanavian writers, such as Knut Hamsun and Johan Bojer, and Russian writers such as Tolstoy and Dostoyevsky. During his senior year, Joe started a correspondence with a fellow aspiring writer named Warren Huddleston. Kalar confided to his kindred spirit that his ideas and readings were creating tension at home:

> My parents are gross materialists—thinking that a full belly is the ultimate goal of every man—and every man that looks for something else is a fool. They sneer and jeer at me because I read Shakespear willingly—and call me a fool because I spend my money for books instead of candy or clothes. "Go," they tell me, "earn your money, and save it, so that when you are old you will have something to fall back upon." Damn, say I. Why should I make myself old trying to save something for my old age? I have youth—and it shall be spent in a youthful way. I will love madly and drink recklessly, and no man can say I am wrong.[8]

As valedictorian of his graduating class, Joe was offered the chance to deliver the commencement address. To prove his point about youth, he initially proposed a defense of Poe's alcoholism, but—when the idea was rejected—delivered instead a bitter rant entitled "The Inferiority Complex of the American People."

That fall, Kalar entered the Bemidji Teachers College. He graduated from the short course with honors and went to teach school in Wayland, a remote spot in western Koochiching County—so remote, in fact, that the only accessible route to the settlement crossed into Canada and back. He taught kindergarten through eighth grade in a one-room log schoolhouse, heated through the brutal winters by a single woodburning barrel stove. Tucked in the heart of timber country in the furthest corner of the state, Kalar felt out of place. He had grown up in tiny International Falls, but nothing had prepared him for the isolation and loneliness of this place. In an unpublished story entitled "Swamp People," he wrote, through the voice of his narrator Mary, of the odd dichotomy of a claustrophobic landscape and distant neighbors:

> We lived on a fertile ridge following the Tamarack river, a small tepid stream that flowed quietly between high banks toward Lake Superior, and all around us, for many miles, stretched the dark lonely muskeg, carpeted with moss, its spruce and tamaracks standing thickly in water. . . . The homesteaders clung to the high ridge, their shacks as far as seven miles apart, with a deep forest between. Our nearest neighbor was half a mile away, beyond a small stretch of muskeg that poked its way like a finger between our shack and his.[9]

To escape the narrow confines of Minnesota, Kalar decided he had to see the country and find his own place in it. He quit teaching after only one year and started hoboing around. He spent a month with friends near Cincinnati, a short time in California, then his longest stint in Chicago. Each place he looked for newspaper work, but no one was hiring. In Chicago, he spent his days riding the streetcars and taking in the seedier side of the city. He claimed, in a sketch written about the time, to have "tramped around the niggersection and fell in love with a highyeller" and "hung around West Madison listening to bums and oystermouthed pimps and homos tried to pick me up and followed me all over Lincoln Park and down Michigan Blvd."[10] He also remembered spending his days in the Argus Bookshop thumbing through books but not having any money to buy. He wrote, "O I didn't go hungry. I had a friend and he was kind of looking out for me though he kept track of how much I owed him figuring that I'd pay him back later when my ship came in but he was nice about it and we'd talk a lot about our schooldays together until we both got lonesome for the dump back in Minnesota with its sawmill and papermill and blindpigs as a man does that's down and out."[11]

In the summer of 1926, Kalar returned to International Falls a defeated man, and took a job in the sawmill as a scaler. Every day he sat in a shack by the entrance gate to the mill, estimating the board feet in each load of lumber before it went into storage, keeping track of the totals for each type of timber. He worked twelve-hour shifts, six days a week.[12]

That summer the young Meridel Le Sueur traveled from Minneapolis to the northern part of the state to write her piece "Evening in a Lumber Town" for *New Masses*. She described the effects of the grinding labor that sawmill workers like Kalar faced, as she watched them "come from the mill, down the streets close together, huddled together. Their black loose clothes are all alike. Like a dark moving mass they come shuffling along heavily, heads lowered, arms hanging, their dark half-drunken faces thrust out. They look drunk, drunk with a deadening concentration."[13] More than the long hours and backbreaking work, Le Sueur lamented the relentless poverty of the lumber camps, which seemed to stunt all emotion and individuality. "They do not celebrate their being," she wrote. "They adhere so closely to the terrible, natural things that they are impersonalized, nullified," but she remained hopeful for the future as night fell and she saw "the very young men come out boldly upon the streets, lean as wolves." She spied a hunger in them that had not yet been defeated: "Genius might spring from such men, from such spare soil—genius too is born of such stark necessity, a humble necessity, a despair. Despair and humbleness make good ground for hardy growth."[14]

Among the lean, young men on the night streets of International Falls was Joseph Kalar, and his own slow realizations of that time make Le Sueur's word seem prophetic. When the promise of shorter hours for better wages seemed far away, Kalar hit the town drinking and womanizing, but soon he recognized that they could not ease his restlessness. He wrote Huddlestone, "I can not find escape from myself in drink, in women . . . only in books can I find surcease of this damnable gnawing."[15] Since graduating from high school he had been assembling a loose group of poems he called "Seed," after his favorite literary magazine of the time. As the year drew to a close, his work began to show vast improvement as he left behind his Romantic influences and began to write about the people and places he knew so well. He wrote one poem entitled "My Village (South International Falls)," another called "Architect" about a drunken hobo building "a castle out of the clay / that banked the ditch," and his first truly autobiographical poem, "The Way It Goes," in which he described himself as

> This one dark-haired
> with a face white like a saint's
> and the thin small girl-like hands
> of a never-has-worked-hard.
> Folks smiled, proud of him.
> Called him prodigy, said he would be a poet.
> That was before his face became pimpled
> and he drank booze
> and sang dirty songs with drunken whores.

Despite these advances in his subject matter, he continued to feel frustrated by the limitations of the form as he knew it. "I try to write poetry . . . it seems good to me," he wrote. "It lays around for awhile . . . I read it over, and it stinks . . . stinks of mediocrity, of artificiality." He began to explore more immediate forms in his writing, most notably the genre he dubbed the "proletarian sketch."

The form was simple, he told Huddlestone; just write "some autobiographical stuff, in a realistic tone, dealing with some specific incident of your life, told in straight autobiographical style skillfully enhanced by creativeness."[16] The advantage of the form, in part, was that it could "combine, as the short story never can, the elements of poetry and the novel."[17] However, as Douglas Wixson writes, the sketch form also appealed to proletarian writers for the same reason it appealed to Soviet writers of the day: "The plotless nature, the personal-narrative quality of the sketch, preserving accents and idioms, was a form suited to the needs of the nonprofessional writer. . . . Straddling journalism and literature, the sketch can be written quickly; it answers the need for quick production and timeliness."[18] Furthermore, the sketch allowed writers like Kalar to address proletarian issues without either the aesthetic distance implied by poetry or the plot demands of a traditionally constructed piece of fiction.

"Forget the plots," Kalar urged. "Grab a chunk of life and chew it and spew it out again. Life isn't a plot, it just goes on and on and is not culminated by a trick ending, very often."[19]

The first of these sketches, "Mesaba Impressions," appeared in *The New Magazine* in March 1927. But the most important break of his young writing career occurred more than a year later when Michael Gold, sympathetic to rebel poets and worker-writers, took editorial control of *New Masses* in June 1928. In his first year as editor, Gold published Kalar's sketches "Midnight Mission," "Proletarian Geography," "Comic Relief in Sawdust," and "Teamsters." At long last, it seemed that he had a champion—just as his work was coming into maturity.

This newfound success revived Kalar's dreams of leaving Minnesota to pursue a life as a writer. Over the summer of 1928 he traveled to the Idaho State Prison in Boise to see the place where Joe Hill was executed, a trip that inspired "Flagwaver," a caustic poem written in what Walter Kalaidjian describes as "the reactionary vernacular of the American midwest":[20]

> When I get patriotic, I go on the big drunk.
> I cut Wesley Everest, I hang that black Injun
> Frank Little from a bridge, I put Joe Hill
> against a wall and fill the lousy bastard
> with hot jets of lead . . .

Around the same time, Kalar began experimenting with using these same sorts of slang terms, even racial slurs, to capture the language of the working class and create what Cary Nelson has called Kalar's own "particularly savage brand of cultural satire."[21]

In the title poem to his 1985 collection *Sweet Will*, Philip Levine described a drunken punch press operator at Detroit Transmission who climbed

> on his wooden soda-pop case to
> his punch press and hollered at all
> of us over the oceanic roar of work,
> addressing us by our names and nations—
> "Nigger, Kike, Hunky, River Rat,"
> but he gave it a tune, an old tune,
> like "America the Beautiful." And he danced . . . .[22]

More than fifty years earlier, Kalar was experimenting with the same approach—often using "bohunk," "gypo," "wop," "nigger," and other racial epithets to describe his fellow workers. He recognized, as Levine did, the equalizing power of these words, and just as the string of slurs comes to sound like "America the Beautiful," so Kalar concludes in "Mesaba Impressions":

> What the hell kind of a country is this, anyway, where a man can't even tell another man what he is? Haven't our ancestors fought for the freedom of speech?
> To the fellow Slovenians, Croats, Finns, Wops, Russians, my love. By God! you showed them that your blood was redder than the iron ore, eh?

Such a tack both satirizes this language and uses it as a way of creating a sense of place and character. Armed with this brand of gritty realism, Kalar continued on from Boise to Seattle, Los Angeles, and Tijuana, writing sketches about each city, two of which ("Seattle: Skidway" and "Tia Juana") appeared in *New Masses*.[23]

When he returned to International Falls in late 1928, Kalar took a job as a mechanic in the papermill, but the success of his trip west gave him hope that he could parlay his travels into sketches and magazine articles. Then, during the summer of 1929, Kalar's father fell seriously ill, and he felt obliged to stay by his side. He wrote Walt Carmon at *New Masses*:

> My old man lies on his bed, horribly swollen. His eyes are puzzled. He can't understand this thing being done to him. Death comes creeping nearer—it is not as Carl Sandburg asked, let it come quick and easy. I can write nothing. My mind refuses to function. I can think only of a proletarian, 53 years old, lying on his bed, looking at the ceiling with puzzled eyes. It isn't fashionable anymore to love one's family: but I am so much a part of it, and I admire my old man so much, that it hurts.[24]

On June 21, 1929, Joe's father, John A. Kalar Sr., died. Kalar's only elder brother had recently married, so the responsibility for supporting his mother and eight younger siblings fell to him alone.

Two hundred miles west in Holt, Minnesota—"a stone's throw from International Falls as eternity goes," Kalar later remembered—poet and printer Ben Hagglund was starting the leftist publication *Western*

Poetry, later renamed *The Rebel Poet.*[25] At a time when it seemed he might never leave International Falls, Kalar must have been glad to see such a magazine start up in his neck of the woods and he liked the first issues enough to send poems to Hagglund. However, his chief advocate, Mike Gold, seemed to be growing increasingly interested in work that was either wholly aesthetic or overtly political. In September 1929 Kalar wrote to Gold to voice his concerns about the recent issues of *New Masses:*

> What I would like to see is a *New Masses* that would be read by lumberjacks, hoboes, miners, clerks, sectionhands, machinists, harvesthands, waiters—the people who should count to us more than paid scribblers. . . . Workers don't write often, they write because if they didn't they would explode. It might be crude stuff—but we're just about done primping before a mirror and powdering our shiny noses. Who are we afraid of?[26]

Not long after, the nation's faltering economy failed utterly. The stock market crashed in October and November, and the country was plunged into the Great Depression. Any lingering dreams of escaping the mills of International Falls were dashed forever.

In the spring of 1930, Kalar moved to South International Falls, then named Holler, where he found a job as a lumberworker. When Mike Gold suggested that Kalar write about the lumber industry, he responded in the pages of *New Masses:*

> I can't see myself doing it. It would be too hard. It is true that I have worked at the lumber "trade" for years—first punching the clock when I was 12 years old—but I have found that it is almost impossible for me to write of it—everything I have tried proved to be abortive. As a matter of fact—ten hours spent on the job would hardly give one the enthusiasm to write about it—for ten hours irons out even the bitterness and hate—leaving only an arid apathy and a desire for "escape". . . . Anyway: today I am a lumberworker, tomorrow the boss may discover the sarcastic opinion I have of him, and I'll be something other than a lumberworker. And so on. We work because we have to, not because we love our jobs—today a lumberworker, tomorrow a ditchdigger, an insurance agent, a clerk, a papermill worker, or gandydancer—we take what we can get.[27]

Yet, even as he claimed that he found it "impossible" to write about the sawmills and papermills of Minnesota, Kalar seemed to be following Gold's advice. In the spring issues of *New Masses* alone, he published the sketch "A Miner's Kid" and the poems "Now that Snow Is Falling" and "Prosperity Blues"—all taking his poor upbringing and bleak future as their central subjects.

That same spring Kalar sent his poem "Invocation to the Wind" to the fledgling Albuquerque journal *Morada*. Editor Norman Macleod not only accepted the poem but called on Kalar to respond to a letter that would appear in the Spring 1930 issue from Ezra Pound. In the letter, Pound referred to the proletariat as "that part of the population engaged solely in reproduction of the human species" and ridiculed the attempts of worker-writers like Kalar to unionize and mobilize a "population too grovelling servile to maintain the status of organism bequethed it by his forbears."[28] The contents of the letter must have hardened Kalar's resolve against aesthetes like Pound and T. S. Eliot.

In his response he lambasted Pound for having "retreated into classicist isolation, absorbed in color and music and words to the exclusion of life and reality." Contrary to Eliot's assertion that twentieth-century poetry must "become more and more comprehensive, more allusive, more indirect," Kalar argued that "new proletarian literature" must be "direct" and "honest."[29] The following year he would further elaborate on these thoughts in a review written for *The Rebel Poet* of their 1931 *Unrest* anthology. In his article, Kalar praised poems that were "suited to our purpose" but looked with "a dubious eye" at more mainstream contributions, particularly Sherwood Anderson's poem "Machine Song." Kalar wrote:

> Aside from being a purely personal acceptance of the machine as the new motivating force in modern "civilization" as contrasted to a former anarchical "opposition" to the machine, the poem has very little concrete value for us. Anderson has not yet seen that machinery to be beautiful must be a servant of the proletariat—to him machinery is as yet but a new esthetic postulate. It is not enough to chant the beauties of machinery without taking into account the realities of the "new life" bred by the machine under capitalism. Only a white collar "stiff" or a leisure-class "artist" can find beauty in a machine as an abstract entity—for a true appreciation of the machine one must go to the worker who manipulates it for wages.[30]

Ironically, even as Kalar was publicly arguing against the Modernists, he was clearly influenced by their work. In his book *American Culture Between the Wars*, Walter Kalaidjian highlights the extent to which Kalar was influenced by—and in turn interrogated—his Modernist forebears, as in his poem "Warm Day in Papermill Town":

> . . . sulfur dioxide
> burns the nose and wreathes the mind
> with thoughts of beaters to be filled,
> pumping jordans, swish swish of hot rolls,
> paper to be made, the crash of spruce,
> furred branches stabbing here and here,
> the arm caught pulpy in the rolls,
> the finger lost; faces young, floating in steam,
> shouting, cursing, seen now,
> haggard in the sun, remembering flowers.

As Kalaidjian astutely suggests, "echoing the 'apparition' of faces in Pound's 'In a Station of the Metro,' Kalar's 'faces young, floating in steam' lends a political inflection to modern imagist poetics."[31] Kalar employs exactly the same technique, and image, in another poem of this period, "Poolroom Faces," which begins: "Faces floating in a poolroom fog, / faces flowering out of collars." While he clearly intends to conjure Pound's poem, he is also intent on reimagining that scene in a setting more familiar to him. In Kalar's world, faces do not only float in the crowd of the Paris Metro but also in the papermills and poolhalls of International Falls.

This tension between imagism's haunting portraits and the harsh language and daily realities of milling towns runs throughout Kalar's poetry. He balances the linguistic experimentation he so admired in e. e. cummings with the more rhetorical and incantatory rhythms of Carl Sandburg and Walt Whitman. Perhaps Kalar's first great influence was Sherwood Anderson's *Winesburg, Ohio*—a book about small-town life and working-class people—but Kalar also admired Anderson's own Whitman-inspired poetry in *Mid-American Chants* and *A New Testament*. At his best Kalar was able to move fluidly from one style to another, to use a cummings-style collision of words like "redwhiteblue frenzy" in the poem "Flagwaver," then turn toward the brash vernacular of

> Let me tell you—
> patriotism is a shot of snow, a whiff of opium,
> a mouthful of rotgut strong enough
> to eat the brass pants off a monkey.

While Kalar clearly held cummings in the highest regard among the Modernist poets—and also greatly admired his novel *The Enormous Room,* which he told Huddlestone was "a warm beautiful mad intense book with prose more marvelous than poetry"[32]—he soon began to distrust the linguistic and syntactical inventions cummings seemed to embody. In his essay "Radicals & Modernists," the British Beat poet Jim Burns asserts:

> What is obvious is that Kalar used techniques taken from the Modernists, but did so in order to accent the fragmentation of society as economic factors caused job losses, evictions, family breakdown, and other social ills. What he said was clear enough, though the way he said it may have seemed strange to those more at home with conventional metric forms, obvious rhymes, and the general traditions of verse making.[33]

During the summer of 1930, hard times hit northern Minnesota and Kalar again found himself "among the unemployed now that 'his' mill has shut down."[34] He went to work for his brother at an insurance agency, and soon had his eye on a legal secretary and court stenographer named Elvena Caple who worked nearby. Nearly four decades later Elvena remembered, "I went out with him but considered him too old—almost six years older than I, too cynical and with not much of a future. I kept turning him down but he always came back."[35] Almost as doggedly as he was pursuing Elvena, Joe was also documenting the plight of the unemployed in International Falls. From the fall of 1930 throughout 1931, he published the finest work of his career, including the poems "After the Storm," "Papermill," "Bank," "Poolroom Faces," and "Warm Day in Papermill Town," and the sketches "Dust of Iron Ore," "Unemployed Anthology," "A Job in the Kraftmill," and "My Uncle Was a Miner."

His sudden burst continued into early 1932 and to the publication of "Worker Uprooted" in the February issue of *New Masses,* but increasingly Mike Gold was losing control of the journal, where Kalar saw that the editorial board "expects, curiously enough, not only a proletarian mirroring in objectivity of facts, but wants, as well, a militancy, revolutionary verve, real or artificial, in the proletarians it writes about. I have a different conception of proletarian literature; I demand, first of all, truth, a mirror of all forms of proletarian experience. And it is artificial to expect a revolutionary orgasm in every proletarian erection."[36] The timing of the shift at *New Masses* was bitterly absurd for Kalar; that very fall, as Mike Gold was giving up control of the magazine utterly, Kalar was starting to work again at the sawmill after a two-year shutdown. He told Huddlestone, "I am now working ten hours a day, which means that 13 hours are wasted as far as anything creative is concerned, and 24 hours practically." The mill would run for three months solid, seven days a week, twenty-four hours a day, "so I'll be unable to do much, and in that sense, I am a real proletarian writer, writing in odd moments when I just have to write."[37]

Writing under such conditions made it difficult for Kalar to achieve the concentration he required for poetry, so he wrote increasingly in the sketch form. During this time he was also turning toward the savage naturalism of the Russian writers he was reading, especially Maxim Gorky. He wrote Huddlestone, "Gorky is my conception of a genius and of all the writers I have aped and wish to ape and will in the future ape, there is none I want to ape more than Gorky. I'd give all the modern writers for the works of Gorky. Modern writers write at life, Gorky writes from life . . . and beautifully, too."[38] Gorky's prose balanced lyrical intensity with brutal realism, offset moments of beauty with careful attention to the detritis of the world. Reading his novels had a profound effect on Kalar's sketches. Consider, for example, the opening of Gorky's *Creatures That Once Were Men:*

> In front of you is the main street, with two rows of miserable-looking huts with shuttered windows and old walls pressing on each other and leaning forward. The roofs of these time-worn habitations are full of holes, and have been patched here and there with laths; from underneath them project mildewed beams, which are shaded by the dusty-leaved elder-trees and crooked white willow—pitiable flora of those suburbs inhabited by the poor.[39]

Compare Gorky's prose with the opening of Kalar's sketch "Unemployed":

> In the shadow of a poolhall he stands limply. It will soon be night. Twilight now is a soft fall of grey ashes. Look: twilight is a dry fog settling on brothels, falling on blindpigs, falling on poolhalls, cigar-stores, cafes. It will soon be night. Darkness creeps stealthily over the papermill, blotting piles of broken lumber, blotting boxcars, piles of sulfite screenings, blotting junkpile, ashpile, coalpile. It will soon be night.

Unfortunately, the lyric density of Kalar's prose sometimes made him a target for those who wished to question the proletarian project. In the pages of the *New York World-Telegram,* the famed reviewer Heywood Broun ridiculed Kalar's story "Night Piece" in a column about the premier issue of *The Anvil.* Broun scoffed at the notion that workers would read Kalar's writing and understand it.[40] The irony, as Walt Kalaidjian has pointed out, is that Kalar was "one of the few proletarian poets of the Depression era who actually earned his living as a mill worker,"[41] a fact that often seemed to cut both ways for Kalar. He was rarely political enough for the revolutionaries, but he was often championed by supporters of the proletarian writers solely because he was a worker, not because of his skill as a writer. At no time was this more apparent than in April 1933, when a selection of Kalar's poems appeared in Mike Gold's anthology *We Gather Strength.* Ousted from *New Masses,* Gold had decided to feature a handful of his favorite poets in what he envisioned as a series of proletarian anthologies. *We Gather Strength* featured Herman Spector, Kalar, Edwin Rolfe, and Sol Funaroff—positioning Kalar as the sole worker-writer.

The anthology featured several of Kalar's best poems and introduced him to a broader audience—including Nelson Algren who considered the book a major influence[42]—but as usual Gold accented Kalar's working-class status and downplayed his abilities as a poet. In the introduction, he wrote:

> Joseph Kalar is a young lumber worker and paper mill mechanic of Minnesota. There is power in him that has not yet found words; but nobody can easily miss the ardor, the fierce proletarian groping for a clue to the world, the painful cheated sense of beauty . . . all, all the new tangled stuff that makes up the proletarian poet's mind. What is he fighting against? What does he want? The battleground is thick in smoke. This poet is a mystic, invoking the strong mysterious wind, or lost in wonder because snow is falling on the planet. He is a mystic, and he works in a papermill, sweating and starving. This is the contradiction, and this is the secret of his Communism.[43]

Even in his praise, Gold was condescending. Not only did he say that Kalar's power "has not yet found words," but, by repeatedly calling him a "mystic," he seemed to imply that Kalar's potency resulted from some exalted proletarian state, rather than from well-crafted poetry. Worse yet, this mystical interpretation misses the point entirely.

When Gold described Kalar as "lost in wonder because snow is falling on the planet," he was referring to the poem "Now that Snow Is Falling." Yet that poem concludes:

> . . . a man walks by us clad thinly, shivering,
> hungry, vainly searching for bread,
> a job, and warm fires; what can we say,
> if such a man passes us bowed against
> the wind, and another, and yet more,
> until he is as a multitude, a sad parade
> of hungry, cold, vague faces? What can we
> say, now that snow is falling?

This is not a poem about being lost in the wonder of nature, but rather a pleading inquiry, asking the reader what we should do now that the growing numbers of hungry and unemployed would be facing another winter.

What seems to have impressed Gold most were not Kalar's gifts as a poet, but rather his potential impact as a political symbol. As Kalaidjian writes, "From Gold's proletcult perspective, Kalar's strength lay in his everyday familiarity with working-class existence coupled with an understanding of Marxism and the Soviet Revolution. His proletarian credentials made him a native son of the American left, one who seemed to embody Gold's Soviet ideal of the worker correspondent."[44]

Unfortunately, casting Kalar as the "Soviet ideal" too often meant setting aside the realities of his life. Gold described Kalar as "a mystic, and he works in a papermill," though Kalar hadn't worked in a papermill in more than three years. He portrayed Kalar as an unfocused worker, asking "What is he fighting against? What does he want?"—when, at the very moment *We Gather Strength* was published, Kalar was organizing the Sawmill Workers Union in hopes of striking for better hours and wages.

In May 1933, the strike "went flat with the abruptness of a punctured tire."[45] The result was more harsh reality for Kalar. He went back to work for ten hours a day at twenty-four cents an hour, usually working the graveyard shift, when the rest of the town was sleeping. More than a year earlier, Warren Huddlestone had sent Kalar a poem entitled "Night-Shift," a poem Kalar greatly admired. His suggestions for revision, however, were significant:

Could you wind it up in true revivalist style and inject a revolutionary resentment at the close of it; inject a bit of hate, a bit of hope, a
hint of the dawn coming, in it. Through the fog of sleep and weariness and muscles aching and cry sleep sleep, make a ray of light shine
with a promise of new dawn? Let us say we work nights, let us say
night-shift carves off great slices of dreams from us, let us say: these
are the doped hours; but let us curse a bit too. Get the idea, kid?[46]

He had concluded by promising, "Eventually, I'll write a night-shift
too," and now the subject was again weighing heavily on his mind.
At the end of August when the shifts were reduced to eight hours,
Kalar told Huddlestone, "Ten hours a day, Jesus, but it was bad, a nig-
gardly counting of minutes and hours of sleep lost in debauchery and
love, wishing, wanting, praying only for sleep, sleep." He began work
on the poem that he had urged Huddlestone to undertake. The first
stanza of Kalar's "Night-Shift" reads:

Sleep aches in the eyes; taste of ashes
dryly sands the mouth, while lips are cracked
with mouthing gobs of stale brown plug;
hours have no periods, no precision, they
are merely hours, stretching into dawn
like a haze of fog greyly lifting over lumber
to warm compulsion of the sun; they are merely
the aching cry of the body for sleep, sleep,
sweet, sweet Jesus, sleep, sleep, the far cry
of drowsy tired blood: sleep, sleep, sleep.

Even the end of the Minneapolis Teamsters' strike in August—a
union victory in Minnesota at last—must have seemed bittersweet. It
came after more than three months of bloody battles and martial law
in the streets of the city. During a riot on one July night, the police
opened fire on the strikers, killing two men and wounding nearly
sixty more. Meridel Le Sueur wrote movingly of the struggle in the
pages of *New Masses* in her dispatches "Murder in Minneapolis" and
"We Were Marching." However, Le Sueur's call to arms had to seem
unrealistic to Kalar and other unionists in more remote parts of Minnesota. It had taken the efforts of thousands—some of whom gave
their lives—a period of months with careful orchestration to win this
single battle. Kalar would never be able to muster such resources or
support.

In September, Kalar's hours were reduced, but by then the relentless work had taken its toll, and he sank into a deep depression. He told Huddlestone that he had "worked, tried desperately to save money, felt myself disintegrate into dull pieces of unimaginative meat, content to fornicate and booze and sleep, reading nothing, writing nothing, caring little." He began drinking heavily. That month, positive reviews of *We Gather Strength* appeared in *International Literature* and *Poetry*. In the pages of *The New Republic,* Isidor Schneider exalted, "For Americans the publishing of *We Gather Strength* is an event worth dating." Schneider was critical of the lack of anger in all the poets, but he specifically praised Kalar as "a writer with vivid sensations" and "confident strength," whose "anger is stronger, his indignation over the deformities of injustice in a world that might be beautiful is sharper and clearer and has a more heroic accent."[47]

Kalar, however, was too consumed to care about the praise. He wrote to Huddlestone, "Last two Saturday nights found Joseph abominably drunk. My hair down over my eyes, I walked the street cursing loudly and in response to friendly salutations I would shout 'Fuck you!' Last Saturday I was unconscious for three hours, tho I walked without staggering, and am now terribly ashamed of myself. Jojo reminds himself of Dmitri in the Brothers Karamozov these days."[48] The drinking soon led to "severe dissension" between Joe and Elvena, which left him, he told Huddlestone, "in a sweating and mad blue funk."[49]

For a short time, he combated the loneliness by working on "Night-Shift" and two new poems, "Repentant Judas"—an impassioned critique of the union bosses who had agreed to the ten-hour shifts—and "Proletarian Night," which Douglas Wixson has called a description of the "feverish dream-state of the exhausted worker-writer." Wixson writes:

> In the proletarian night when other workers enjoyed the sleep of those whose jobs did not require them to think . . . worker-writers were reconstructing a world of work in their writing, drawing upon the materials of the day's experiences, the fugitive exchanges between workers, the small and grand strokes of workers' existences, searching for and recovering the "folk" in transformed settings. In the fitful nights between days of labor, the worker-writer "dreams" the work world. The proletarian night is another name for the worker-writer's dual consciousness.[50]

Kalar's last poems reveal not only this duality, but also the exhaustion of this double life; they show his waning faith in the power of poetry to transform social injustice and his deepening doubts about the value of his efforts.

Kalar was not alone. In the past year Ben Hagglund, finally fed up with the "lunatic" farmers of Holt, Minnesota, had moved to New-llano, Texas, then given up printing *The Anvil*. The magazine struggled another year but finally folded in 1935. Tillie Olsen (then Tillie Lerner), who had been living in Faribault, Minnesota, working on her novel *Yonnondio*, fled the state under circumstances she would never fully discuss; shortly after the first chapter of her novel-in-progress appeared in the February 1934 premiere issue of *Partisan Review*, interested publishers had to spring her from jail.

The depth of Kalar's own disillusionment is apparent in a brief autobiographical piece composed for *International Literature*, in which he complains that discussions of proletarian literature and decisions about the movement's artistic direction were always determined by writers in the cities. "Nothing whatever has been said about the writer in a small town," he wrote, "a writer with broad revolutionary sympathies, forced to live almost an isolated intellectual existence." Worse yet, Kalar was visibly discouraged by the reviews of *We Gather Strength*, which praised the poems he believed were weakest and criticized his best work because it did not fit these ideals determined by urban intellectuals. Such critiques, he worried, forced the rural writer to become

> less rooted to the local realities and his creative work tends toward an abstract internationalism that may be very fine as far as the particular work in question is concerned, but dangerous to the writer. As in my poems, "Invocation to the Wind," "Now that Snow Is Falling," "After the Storm," you will note an evasion of local realities by substituting an internationalism or recreation of the past. It is a significant point that the two poems dealing with local realities, "Papermill" and "Poolroom Faces," have been characterized as defeatest, passive, etc., etc. The comrades must take these things into consideration in dealing with a writer "in the sticks."[51]

By 1935 Kalar had given up entirely. His poem "Thunder in a Moment of Calm" appeared in *The Anvil* in May, just weeks after his twenty-ninth birthday. It was the last new poem he ever published.

Kalar was turning decidely away from his artistic pursuits and toward a normal, middle-class life. Three months earlier, he had taken a job in the office at the sawmill "with the same pay and our feet hoisted on our desks half the time and me spouting red vituperation."[52] He had reconciled with Elvena, and they were engaged to be married. On September 5, 1935, just ten days before their wedding, Kalar wrote Huddlestone a long letter mourning his lost youth:

> As I look back I seem to have been quite a lusty roistering sort of chap who avoided good jobs with almost fanatical intentness, who worked five or six months and then pulled tail for here or there and in the meantime boozed, cursed, wrote poems, and lay around in a somnolent paralysis. Look at the bastard now, pooped out, too tired to write, to feel the glow of anger, too tired to read, to respond to the plunging line, dopey, stupid, a fit swine for the manure pile. And to top it off the swine not content with moral and mental degeneration of a job is firmly determined in a fattish complacent sort of way to enter the old soldiers home of matrimony Sept. 15. Only distantly do I feel reverberations of revolt against what is known as manifest destiny, for the greater part, I march docilely to slaughter, my pecker hanging out and my eyes with the dead empty look of two chamberpots under a bed.[53]

When asked by Huddlestone in November if he intended to publish a book, Kalar replied, "Yes I have often thought of getting out a booklet of my stuff. . . . I haven't put it together yet anyway, but eventually, as a sort of obituary, I intend to do it." He even had interest from James Henle at Vanguard Press—the premiere publisher of young Communist writers. In addition to issuing daring books ranging from radical economic theory to informational pamphlets about abortion, from exposés of health violations in the food industry to a "handbook for hoboes," Vanguard's stable of authors included Upton Sinclair, Nelson Algren, Vardis Fisher, Dr. Seuss, and their workhorse, James T. Farrell. Henle urged Kalar to "send on my stuff and I like a swine didn't do it."[54]

Two months later, Ben Hagglund "finally broke down" and asked Kalar for a manuscript of poems to print as part of a pamphlet series he had started in Newllano, Texas. Kalar wrote Huddlestone:

> I took inventory of my creative harvest and found to my chagrin that the total product of my hand which I view now without becoming to-

tally overwhelmed by the stench comprises in all 16 poems. Frankly, I was dismayed. With a fat sort of complacency I had imagined that I had a long and honorable creative past behind me; the meagerness stunned me. So I turned Ben down until the old machine begins to work again.[55]

The "old machine" of Kalar's creativity never did begin again. After years of battling the front offices of his various mills, Kalar accepted the job of establishing an Industrial Relations Department for the International Lumber Company. In 1939, he ran unsuccessfully for State Representative of the 62nd district, but the following year he became head of the entire Personnel and Labor Relations Department of International Lumber. In late 1954, he was transferred to the main office in Minneapolis, where he served as a member of the Insulite sales staff until he retired in 1967.

Three years into his retirement, Kalar received a letter from Jack Salzman, who was assembling an anthology of radical poetry (published eight years later as *Social Poetry of the 1930s*). He requested permission to reprint twelve of Joe's poems. Kalar happily agreed, but found:

In looking over some of these poems, some of which I haven't looked at for over 30 years, the conviction is reaffirmed that these were not written by Jojo at all but by an entirely different person. Some of the corny phrasing approaches the worst levels of camp, errors in construction are very apparent and in spots I even plagiarize from my own works. However, I suppose they might be interesting, despite all their faults, to the people who are interested in turning over the dusty years of that time.[56]

On February 23, 1972, Joseph Kalar died unexpectedly in his Minneapolis home. He was two months shy of his sixty-sixth birthday. His obituary in the *International Falls Journal* made mention of his forty-five years of work in sawmills and papermills but contained no reference to his writings. Elvena remembered, "The boys and I were just sick because we didn't know where any of [his work] was. I thought it was all in the publications. I didn't have any idea where to look. I started writing to other writers and old friends of his to locate it. . . . We did find a lot of his writings. I have no idea how much of it we do have."[57]

In the early 1980s, with the assistance of Douglas Wixson, Kalar's son, Richard, gathered a number of the missing pieces and put together a collection of Kalar's poems, stories, sketches, and letters, of which one hundred copies were privately printed and distributed to family members. Scarce and highly coveted by scholars, that collection, *Joseph A. Kalar: Poet of Protest,* has remained the sole printed resource, until now.

ℰ⌒

Joseph Kalar's artistic career was short but intense. Working in stolen moments found over a period of only a few short years, his poems and sketches are a brief but bright record of a long-neglected era in our literary tradition. Among the worker-writers—that lost branch of American Modernism—Joseph Kalar stands as a kind of northwoods Rimbaud: a brilliant young man and gifted poet, who composed some of the twentieth century's finest poetic portraits of the working class and was then utterly forgotten.

In his introduction to *Repression and Recovery: Modern Poetry and the Politics of Cultural Memory, 1910–1945,* Cary Nelson argues that "we no longer know the history of the poetry of the first half of [the twentieth] century; most of us, moreover, do not know that the knowledge is gone."[58] Indeed, it has only been in the last fifteen years that a groundswell of interest has produced serious inquiry into the 1920s and '30s, especially as concerns fringe writers—writers of color, women writers, worker-writers. "Until recent books by Cary Nelson, Walter Kalaidjian, Michael Denning, and others," Alan M. Wald recently wrote, "the Left avant-garde was perceived as pre-modernist, if not near subliterary."[59]

Certainly, the triple obstacles of World War II, the McCarthy era, and the Vietnam War have, for many years, served to obscure the value of many of the Communist writers of the 1930s. This recent scholarship, however, has at last provided the context and the associations by which to understand the poets and writers of this era. These historical and cultural perspectives help to place Kalar in a central position among the radical writers of his day, but more importantly, the poems continue to speak across time and directly to the twin human emotions of despair and defiance.

Eliot said, "The great poet, in writing himself, writes his time." By that standard, Kalar is certainly one of the most important writers of his time, but far beyond his single, most anthologized poem, his work continues to be essential to understanding one of the greatest moments of crisis in our national history. Perhaps better than any other record we have, Joseph Kalar's writings both document the personal struggles of a particular worker-writer and reflect the era during which the souls of all working Americans were most sorely tested.

Notes

1. Cary Nelson, "A Sheaf of Political Poetry in the Modern Period" in *Heath Anthology of American Literature*, Vol. 2, ed. Paul Lauter (Lexington, Mass.: D. C. Heath and Co., 2nd ed., 1994), 1391.

2. Quoted in Richard G. Kalar, ed., *Joseph A. Kalar: Poet of Protest* (Minneapolis, Minn.: RGK Publications, 1985), 298.

3. Kalar to Huddlestone, 28 September 1967; 6 May 1936. This and subsequent citations of Kalar's letters refer to manuscript letters in the collection of Richard Kalar.

4. Robert Shulman, *The Power of Political Art: The 1930s Literary Left Reconsidered* (Chapel Hill: University of North Carolina Press), 19.

5. Kalar to Warren Huddlestone, 5 September 1935.

6. See Joe Paddock, *Keeper of the Wild: The Life of Ernest Oberholtzer* (St. Paul: Minnesota Historical Society Press, 2001).

7. "A Symposium—Where We Stand: Joseph Kalar," *International Literature* (July 1934): 91.

8. Kalar to Huddlestone, 5 February 1924.

9. Richard Kalar, *Joseph A. Kalar*, 105.

10. Ibid., 122.

11. Ibid.

12. Ibid., 338.

13. Meridel Le Sueur, "Evening in a Lumber Town," *New Masses*, (July 1926): 22–23.

14. Ibid.

15. Kalar to Huddlestone, August 1926.

16. Kalar to Huddlestone, 4 September 1932.

17. Kalar to Huddlestone, 6 November 1932.

18. Douglas Wixson, *Worker-Writer in America: Jack Conroy and the Tradition of Midwestern Literary Radicalism, 1898–1990* (Urbana: University of Illinois Press, 1994): 298.

19. Kalar to Huddlestone, 7 December 1932.

20. Walter Kalaidjian, *American Culture Between the Wars: Revisionary Modernism and Postmodern Critique* (New York: Columbia University Press, 1993), 157.

21. Cary Nelson, *Repression and Recovery: Modern American Poetry and the Politics of Cultural Memory, 1910–1945* (Madison: University of Wisconsin Press, 1989), 300.

22. Philip Levine, *Sweet Will* (New York: Atheneum, 1985), 17–18.

23. Wixson, *Worker-Writer*, 140.

24. Richard Kalar, *Joseph A. Kalar*, xi.

25. Kalar to Huddlestone, 13 December 1964.

26. Kalar, "He Wants to Know," *New Masses* (September 1929): 22.

27. Kalar, "On New Program for Writers," *New Masses* (April 1930): 21.

28. *Morada* 3 (Spring 1930): 90–91.

29. Ibid., 91–92.

30. Kalar, review of "Machine Song" by Sherwood Anderson, *Rebel Poet* 10–12 (October-December 1931): 10.

31. Kalaidjian, *American Culture,* 157.

32. Kalar to Huddlestone, 26 September 1932.

33. Jim Burns, "Radicals & Modernists," *Prop* 3 (Summer 1997): 11.

34. "In This Issue," *New Masses* (November 1930): 22.

35. Richard Kalar, *Joseph A. Kalar,* 338.

36. Kalar to Huddlestone, 16 October 1932.

37. Kalar to Huddlestone, 4 September 1932.

38. Kalar to Huddlestone, 7 December 1932.

39. Maxim Gorky, *Creatures That Once Were Men* (New York: Boni and Liveright, 1918), 13.

40. Heywood Broun, "It Seems to Me," *New York World-Telegram* May 15, 1933.

41. Kalaidjian, *American Culture,* 156.

42. See Wixson, *Worker-Writer,* 322.

43. Michael Gold, "Introduction," *We Gather Strength* (New York: Liberal Press, 1933), 7–9.

44. Kalaidjian, *Worker-Writer,* 156.

45. Kalar to Huddlestone, 15 May 1933.

46. Kalar to Huddlestone, 16 October 1932.

47. Isidor Schneider, *The New Republic* (September 13, 1933): 135.

48. Kalar to Huddlestone, 16 September 1933.

49. Kalar to Huddlestone, 3 November 1933.

50. Wixson, *Worker-Writer,* 212.

51. "A Symposium—Where We Stand," 93.

52. Kalar to Huddlestone, 4 February 1935.

53. Kalar to Huddlestone, 5 September 1935.

54. Kalar to Huddlestone, 2 November 1935.

55. Kalar to Huddlestone, 10 January 1936.

56. Kalar to Huddlestone, 7 May 1970.

57. Richard Kalar, *Joseph A. Kalar,* 338–39.

58. Nelson, *Repression and Recovery,* 4.

59. Alan M. Wald, *Exiles from a Future Time: The Forging of the Mid-Twentieth-Century Literary Left* (Chapel Hill: University of North Carolina Press, 2002), 321–22.

I

NIGHT-SHIFT

Sleep aches in the eyes; taste of ashes
dryly sands the mouth, while lips are cracked
with mouthing gobs of stale brown plug;
hours have no periods, no precision, they
are merely hours, stretching into dawn
like a haze of fog greyly lifting over lumber
to warm compulsion of the sun; they are merely
the aching cry of the body for sleep, sleep,
sweet, sweet Jesus, sleep, sleep, the far cry
of drowsy tired blood: sleep, sleep, sleep.

Into the night, body a hunch against darkness,
jostling and bouncing on a wagon rigid
with stiffness, permitting no dreams of cotton,
creaking, groaning, a clot of shadow urgently
propelled down dark canyons of lumber, poking
fragrant load of pine between rows of piles
darkly reminiscent of western canyons of stone,
thoughts swarm drowsily behind the eyes of this man
who stares vacantly at the giant swell and roll
of horse buttocks dark and heaving before him,
thinking no more while muscles bulge terribly
like pistons moving smoothly under hide,
and the body is only a remembered cry for sleep.

In the morning when dawn has crept over the sky,
lips are a thin line not curving into the glow
of a smile, eyes are a lesson in brooding and vision,
and hands clutching at leather reins are ominous
with significance; though sleep is a phlegm of weariness
clothing his mind, hate is knowledge incandescent
bright illumination for a mind busy with planning,
and hands are rich with promise of a tomorrow

in which dreams will sprout beautifully into action,
and throats harsh with cursing will shout terribly
the words that will give meaning to hours,
precision to time, significance to bodies
now but a far painful cry in blood for sleep.

PROLETARIAN NIGHT

Now that work is done, the whistle blows,
its scream harsh as laughter out of steel,
piercing through the fat, pushing aside
the fur, the sleep, the dream,
finding each sad little cringing nerve
twitching in its cell of tired flesh,
while from the stack and the round mouths
of black dripping pipes, smoke puffs,
puffs, and sound dies, and giant wheels
cease their grinding, and pistons find rest
in the slimy clutch of oil and grease.
Now that work is done, the mill no longer
with a drone grinds gold out of flesh,
but with the night and its quiet dark
and sleep that presses on the eyes,
the tumult and the drive persist, and we find
remembrance in each nerve and bone and cell
of the grating sharp insistence of each wheel,
the slap of belts, tumultuous din of steel,
the insolent commands, the curses and the sneers
(with humility such a poor veil to hide
the hate that flames electric into the eyes);
though the body cries for rest, writhing
with aching flesh throughout the night,
and sleep descends with its blind crazy dreams,
stuffing the mind with rags that dull,
conviction, still inviolate, remains,
that will not hail victory in,
remove the steel thumbs of the mill
that gouge into the temples (here and here),
return one beam of lost forgotten day,
or drive one foe into the avenging street.

THE WAY IT GOES

Out of a boozing father
and a bar-maid wife
came a meaningless rhapsody of nine kids . . .
all boys . . . every one of them . . .
and maybe a girl that is dead
and sleeps in the graveyard
and now whimpers with joy on the white bosom of God,
but their eyes don't go salt with tears
when they think of her,
their only daughter dead and an angel.

She was only two days old when she died and the mother
had other things to think of,
then . . .

A rhapsody of nine kids . . .
boys . . . every one of them . . .

This one hard-headed as a Jew,
maybe a Rockefeller . . .
"Come to me, yellow babies, beautiful golden kids,
twenty dollar gold kids . . ."
Muttering,
"Shakespeare, Goethe,
Damn' worthless nuts, both of them."

This one dark-haired
with face white like a saint's
and then thin small girl-like hands
of a never-has-worked-hard.
Folks smiled, proud of him.
Called him prodigy, said he would be a poet.
That was before his face became pimpled

and he drank booze
and sang dirty songs with drunken whores.

Just the way it goes . . .
Just the way it goes . . .
that's all.

Out of a boozing father
and bar-maid for a wife . . .
came a meaningless rhapsody of nine kids . . .
all boys . . . every one of them . . .
this one poet . . . that one pick and shovel man . . .
this one boozer . . .
All of them
out of a boozing father
and a bar-maid for a wife . . .

DUST OF IRON ORE

Iron ore had seeped into sewer creek, a crazy, slimy, little stream that ran beside the railroad tracks right through Chicken Town, coloring it a yellowish red and investing the bits of sewage that bobbed in its tiny currents with a fantastic grandeur. Dust of iron ore, kneaded by the tramp of miners' feet, mixed with the mud on the streets into greyish-red gumbo which plastered itself stickily to shoes and was carried all over the town.

The miners, emerging like bats from shafts leading deep into the earth, were stained red and yellow with it, their clothes streaked and hardened with the dust, from which emanated a peculiar stink of dampness, sweat, and iron ore. I remember how accustomed we became to the stink of work my father carried about with him. It was so much a part of him that, years later, when my father left the pits, we were startled and he seemed unfamiliar, as the iron ore stink slowly left his clothes, to be replaced by a new stink, gathered in the dripping rooms of a papermill. It was something like the time, quite horrible and shameful to us, when he had shaved the black moustache without which he was to us no more than a stranger, frightening us with his blue upperlip, resembling that of a corpse.

The mine was like some horrible monster hidden in the red bowels of the earth, exhaling a poisonous vapor of dust which dropped like an unseen fog over Merritt and the little locations where the miners lived. We knew, dimly, that Merritt belonged to this monster, and that whenever it raged there deep in the earth, some of our fathers, or uncles, or brothers, would be carried out blue in the face with guts swelling over their belts; or at times it got sick, and then there was nothing to eat at home, and our father was a furtive shadow dodging in and out of the house, coming home late at night with a mean snarling temper. We felt that we children belonged to it; we blamed it for all the unpleasant things we had to do; we felt that it was the being that made us go to school just as it made our fathers go to work; and we felt, in a queer fatalistic way, that the rats belonged to this monster as well.

The rats had taken possession of Chicken Town by the thousands, drawn perhaps by the mines, sewer creek, or the stink of iron ore. They were everywhere, large, fat, loathsome. Their ugly heads popped from every hole, studied us with mean, hard, blinking indifferent eyes. Holes were gnawed in chicken coops; chickens were massacred, rabbits were butchered wantonly and maliciously. The rich have Atlantic City in which to disport themselves; the rats, like a new leisure class living on the bounty of the miners, disported themselves in sewer creek, swimming and diving, pouncing on bits of sewage, showing their teeth at us as we threw stones. The miners were indifferent to them. They told fabulous stories of different rats in the mines, gave them good friendly bohunk names, talked of them as though they were pets. Their wives, however, railed and swore at them, strove futilely to stem the swarm by nailing pieces of tin over holes, and called on the Devil to witness the abomination of it. To us, rats were something like snakes; discovered unexpectedly to be peering at us, they made our spines crawl and writhe with a chill scampering of wet mice feet.

The rats became so thick wherever the miners lived that the fat councilman had to make a show of doing something. They offered a bounty of five cents on each dead rat brought to the courthouse. When we heard this news, we all felt as though we had come into an inheritance. This was a matter of business, of filling our pockets with jingling nickels, of getting ahead in the world. We laid plans carefully; our separate gangs became more disciplined.

Rats were slaughtered by the hundreds. Wherever a hole gnawed through a floor indicated a rat might be living there, we dug. We combed the country. We pawed in sewer creek. We used clubs, poison, dogs. It was our joy to come upon a nest with six or seven blind, shivering naked baby rats crawling in it. They were dispatched unmercifully. We loaded them all into a burlap sack. They were carried proudly to the courthouse. Each rat was picked separately out of the sack, caressed by our hands, and laid like a chunk of meat on the floor. Some of them stank foully; it made little difference to us if we picked a corpse out of a garbage pail and it were already disintegrating in the last foul stage of decay. In those moments we almost came to love rats, we no longer shuddered with instinctive aversion, nor felt the running of mice feet up our spines at sight of them.

The dumpground, which held a queer attraction for us, was a popular dwelling ground for rats who found it a communal paradise. They pawed over the reeking juicy garbage, slid and rolled in it. At least twice a day we made the rounds, until one day we came upon something that scared us horribly, and that made us shun the dump for months afterward.

The day was hot; sewer creek steamed and murmured in the sun; the dump with its decaying horses, dogs, and cats, fried with a horrible stench in the sun. We walked slowly, sweat gluing our shirts to our backs. Our little rat terrier, who had an almost neurotic hatred of rats, ran ahead of us, his red tongue a scarlet splash over his jaw. We lost sight of him. Suddenly he began to bark; we stopped amazed and startled, for his bark was that of sudden fright blended into a long mournful howl, such as we had never heard before. We ran, and again stopped, pale with fear.

There before us, in a welter of garbage, lay prone a man, shotgun by his side. He was dead. His feet were bare. His ragged clothes were stained red and yellow with iron ore dust. "A stiff," we whispered, staring with distended eyes at his bare feet, trying to avoid the sight of a congealing pool of blood and brains by his head. For a moment, paralyzed with fear, our eyes glazed by the shock, we stared at him, our lips working convulsively. Then we ran.

We never found out why he shot himself. Our fathers looked askance at us if we questioned. I had nightmares so horrible that I wet the bed in my fear. Nights afterward, in my dreams, I could see thousands of rats pursuing thousands of men who all seemed like my father, shoulders humped, overalls smeared in red and yellow, who ran awkwardly as though crippled; there would be a blinding flash of stabbing light which sent miners and rats swirling around and around like a pin-wheel, finally dissolving and merging them with startling clearness into the form of a man lying wearily on garbage, at whom I stared with eyes filmed with nightmare, and who I recognized to be the man who had chosen a dump on which to die.

FUNERAL

A funeral cortege passing down the street,
quietly, stealthily,
as if ashamed of itself.

—Women wail for lost lovers,
scream for dead husbands,
their streaming hair
piteously wild.

(Beautiful lady:
Do not open your window,
dove-like hands gemmed
with scintillating jewels.
Beautiful lady:
Do not call the footman to see
what the hell is raising such a racket on the street.
It is nothing.
All will soon be quiet again.)

Just another miner,
just another wop,
stench of iron ore on overalls,
hugs the cool brown
maternal earth,
the weight of mountains on his back,
guts oozing redly
over belt buckled at the last hole.

(Beautiful lady:
It is nothing.
All will soon be quiet again.)

WARM DAY IN PAPERMILL TOWN

Now bursts the fat sun into heat,
probing black corners with shafts of light,
feeling out all dark beaten things;
snow rots, and water runs greasily
in gutters; snuffcans, gumwrappers,
cigarettebutts, a few blundering leaves
sail irresolute to dubious seas,
while warm, drooping, haggard in light,
men lean limply on grey buildings,
sniffing the air, remembering flowers,
faded memory of work lurking in dead eyes
appraising women clicking down the walk,
and sparrows, sardonic in wisdom, lunge,
contend fiercely in the grey street.
Stink from papermill, sulfur dioxide,
burns the nose and wreathes the mind
with thoughts of beaters to be filled,
pumping jordans, swish swish of hot rolls,
paper to be made, the crash of spruce,
furred branches stabbing here and there,
the arm caught pulpy in the rolls,
the finger, lost; faces young, floating in steam,
shouting, cursing, seen now,
haggard in the sun, remembering flowers.

GREENLUMBER CHAIN

This is lumber
damp white aromatic
note well orderly regimented procession
pull sweat curse
lumber must be piled to dry.
Watch.
See your hands.
They pull. One two three.
This is the belt.
Onetwothree
onetwothree
say it over and over
roll it with your tongue
like wine
it is not sweet
and when sweat drowns your eyes
feet ache arms sore
think
look at the lumber
say
my life is a nice orderly regimented procession
ask,
why?

SAWDUST

I.

The sawmill lounges woodenly by the river, huge, red, barnlike, snoring with a purr of flying sawdust, shaking under the mad rush of catapulting carriages, throbbing with the sonorous buzzing and whining of saws and edgers. On the landing, the logs roll from flatcars with rumblings of thunder, fall with a terrific splash and spraying of water into the river. The logs, propelled through the hot pond deftly by pikepoles in the hands of slipmen, march up the dripping slip docilely like hogs on slaughtering belts, and are kicked viciously toward the hurtling carriages by wicked thrusts of "niggers" cleverly manipulated by sawyers.

(From the windows the river is seen, tame with the tameness of the very old. The riverbottom is slimy with pitch and bark and sawdust: deep down in the shadows, deadheads, sodden and wetly grey, bob and suck and strain at the tug of the current, releasing a sudden uprush of oily bubbles. The river flows with violent eruptions of foam from Rainy Lake, flows placidly toward the dam, rushes through the gates and splinters into fragments of curled spurts on the rock below, absorbs stink and waste and bark from the papermill, becomes grey with sewage, flows toward Manitou, Spooner, Baudette, past vacant sawmills lounging like rigid carcasses, past rotting piles of sawdust, deserted lumbercamps, hoists, empties into Lake of the Woods.)

In the sawmill the setters crouch on the carriages, bend knees to meet hurtling backward rush, bend knees to meet rush of carriages toward the eager saw. Back and forth; back and forth; back and forth. Jerking of levers three or four times with each mad rush, over and over. Nothing more. Three o'clock in the morning the men look like automatons; their faces are vacant and grey. Arms become levers, legs become steel, faces are sculptured in iron. Legs bending at the knees, men stare vacantly, greyly, mechanically pulling levers, mechanically juggling hooks and pikepoles, grasping lumber from hurrying chains, straightening lumber, picking slabs, sweeping sawdust.

The sawmill lounges woodenly by the river, sawdust its excrement. Men hurry with a swinging of dinnerpails through the gates, disappear into the timeshack, known as Lars Larson, Matt Stefan, John Porokovitch, Tim McManus, punch a clock, emerge as Numbers 707, 615, 214, 332. The sawmill yawns with much belching of rumbling noises: the men march in. They disappear.

Men curse loudly, men curse softly: curses are the blind groping explosions of pained bewilderment. Men curse. It does not matter. Curses cannot be heard above saw whining, edgers screaming, logs thumping with rumblings of thunder on the landing.

II.

The sky is a wet blanket of grey sawdust. The wind throws sawdust into my eyes: I cannot see. The food I eat is sawdust. I am writing with a tired hand: my hand is sawdust. I try to sing bravely: my throat is choked with sawdust. I try to think: my mind is sawdust. I cannot see and I cannot understand.

Yesterday I walked down the road swinging my dinnerpail thinking of pines growing darkly tall on sandy hills, of green poplars growing by small rivers. The road was dusty and the sun was hot. My feet were tired. Lumberpiles cast fantastic shadows on the road. Shadows wavered, lengthened and contracted, flapped like clothes on a line.

Suddenly I stumbled over a rock in the road. I fell. My head hit sharply the edge of the dinnerpail, cutting me deeply. A ball of darkness exploded in my brain. I became unconscious. As I lay limply on the road, a small stream of sawdust trickled from the cut on my forehead, down my cheek, congealing on my lips.

A GYPO IN SAWDUST

As damp aromatic loads of whitepine, norway, spruce, tamarack, poplar, pulled into the lumberyard by sweating, puffing horses pounded on tense gargantuan rumps by cursing teamsters, pass him, he smiles with the imbecile expression of a man winning on the stockmarket, with the blatant joy of a bookkeeper getting a cigar from the boss. Years of piecework have turned him into a cursing vicious automaton, a monomaniac whose nights in bed are made wetly hideous by nightmares of lumberpiles toppling into allies with a madness of flying planks, of skyhigh piling machines remorselessly dropping huge planks on his head, bearing lumber to him so rapidly he cannot take it away.

On warm days the sun beats tenderly on Lars. He is getting old. His body begins to creak. Rotgut and homebrew have ravaged muscles bulging with much hefting of pitch-heavy lumber. "You take a gypo," the dayworkers say, "you take a gypo now. Two or three years they gypo and then they ain't human no more. They get lumber hungry. They never get enough lumber. Look at the way they tears into the loads, like a mad bull tearing the guts out of a dog."

To Lars, life hangs in the balance on the number of feet the scaler has allowed him on the famous blue ticket. So many hundred feet, so many thousand. He looks at the blue ticket, his face becomes red with rage, he roars, "Well, Jesus Christ, is that all that lousy bonus bastard gave us for this load? Well, suffering Christ, it don't pay to pile lumber no more with a stoolpigeon like that!"

When Lars dies heaven will be for him a huge lumberyard basking under an eternal sun; heaven will be for him a huge piling machine creaking skyward slowly with hooks placed five feet apart, each hook bearing a 2 x 10 plank, and on each one a gigantic schooner of beer, damply cool, erupting into white bursts of foam.

TESTAMENT

In the lean earth there is nothing,
Nothing but Life, a ball of horse's dung,
And I, a sparrow.

To my pecking and scratching here, leave me.
Leave me alone now.
Who can tell but that I will find
Some goodly oats to be uncovered here?

THEY BLOW WHISTLES FOR THE NEW YEAR

Forty men, maybe more,
think:
time crawls like a caterpillar,
time is a white worm
boring into steel.

The new year comes like a stallion
in jingling harness
saying:
    Men are flyspecks
    on white parchment of life.
She comes like a fat wench
slow, uncertain of purpose.
It does not matter.
Whistles scream like mares in pain,
tugboats in harbor toot,
foghorns flatulate in dusky dawn.
There shall be much wine spilled on the table today,
and many drunks will be carried out feet first.

Forty men
hearing loud vomit of noise,
stop the wheels of thought.
Forty men, maybe more,
miners, railroadmen, textileworkers,
peering through iron bars,
ask the dawn,
what the hell is all the noise about?
There seems to be no answer.

MESABA IMPRESSIONS

I.

A motley assortment of children screaming to school, Slovenians, Croatians, Roumanians, Finns, Italians, and Russians, trudging trust-fully to the potent fount of education to learn to be better Americans than their parents, step and examine with awe the colossal piles of iron ore, a conglomerate pin-wheel of colors, yellow, red, and orange. Often they would stop and fill their pockets with the ore and then get one hell of a pounding when they got home. It made very good chalk. The watchmen, if they saw them, would shout out, "Hey there, you damned bohunks, get the hell away from there!"

After they got to school they would steal some paper and draw. They were furnished with pencils, by the city, but they always preferred the ore chalk, especially the red. In a way it was symbolical, though they never knew that then. They would draw grotesque men, with big bellies and round heads with the red chalk. They called them Papa, or Uncle Mike, or Grandpa. They were too young then to know that their papas might be brought home any day, crushed, groaning, and red with blood.

II.

A man we all knew well and who was damned good to us kids got killed one day. The papers called it an unfortunate accident. It just happened that the shaft caved in. He sure was hurt some. I guess he only lived long enough to taste the iron ore in his mouth. Anyway his neck was all twisted to hell, his legs were broken, and his bloody guts hung over the tops of his trousers.

My folks went to see the wife of the man. A nice mess, eh? Wife and kids left without an old man, he having been brought home with his insides all out of him. It was a very nice house, too, nice pictures on the wall. There was one showing an old gent with a sheep in his arms on which it said, "The Lord is My Shepherd." Another one showed the same gent on the cross, and it said, "He Died for Man."

When I left, the old lady and kids were bawling to beat all Christ. I couldn't help but howl myself, for I was only eight years old then.

III.

I had an uncle, Mike his name was, who wouldn't work in the mines anymore. He had worked long enough and I suppose he figured that it was time he took a lay-off. He bummed around on freight cars and came home and said, "Believe me it sure is tough bumming around. Don't get anything to eat half the time. Yes, Joe," he would say, laying his hand on my shoulder, "you gotta work to get along in this world." And then the next thing we would know he would be off again, digging ditches in a muskeg near International Falls. When he came back he got a job bartending for Agnich, in Eveleth, where my father always bought his beer. My father would ask him why he wouldn't work in the mines anymore. Mike would just say: "to hell with it!"

Well, he got worse and worse. "Sure," he said, "I'll go and see the sawbones." He would go out and spend the day in the saloon, come home and say, the doc says I'm all right. He coughed more and more, and each time he coughed a bloody piece of his lung would go plunk in the spittoon. He did go to a sanitarium after he wasn't able to walk anymore. I guess when the docs told him he was going to kick the bucket, he says, between coughs: "well, to hell with it!"

You smug bosses, when you've stepped on a man's foot so long that he says "well, to hell with it!"—look out. And Mike, you bohunk, you were all right. I give you my love. I didn't understand you then, thought you were a little bughouse, but I see it now.

IV.

Every Sunday after church a lot of the miners come to our house. Well, we got by this time. The timbers held up pretty good. Then they would drink.

But Christ, I don't know as how you can blame them, working in the shafts and expecting any minute to have the walls cave in on you and mix your guts with the red ore! See your pals, with whom you came over from the old country, carried home, bleeding and groaning, "Jesus, Jesus."

Saturday night coming around, another week. Well, well, we got by this time, eh? Let's celebrate, eh?

The Mesaba strike: No wonder our papa Coolidge and the rest of the good Americans say, Keep those damned furriers out of the country. The dirty bastards, don't know when they've got a good thing. Too flammable. TNT. Any damned long whiskered agitator can stir them up to raise hell. We want America for the Americans. We Nordics—by God! we're the solid men. You can't make us think with our stomachs. Those damned bohunks and wops, Christ you can even call them SOB's before they want to stick you. What the hell kind of a country is this, anyway, where a man can't even tell another man what he is? Haven't our ancestors fought for the freedom of speech?

To the fellow Slovenians, Croats, Finns, Wops, Russians, my love. By God! you showed them that your blood was redder than the iron ore, eh?

V.

To my dear friends, the bosses and owners, the manufacturers and store keepers I say: You are doing wisely when you keep a bohunk's belly full of food. You sure got the grey matter.

I say this just because I remember only too well my days on the Mesaba Range, when times were a little tough, and my mother sent me after bones for the dog to make soup out of, and the mines shut down.

Miners, with the iron ore stink, muttering: "What the hell, men, what the hell?"

REPENTANT JUDAS

When the five o'clock whistle blows,
he comes to stand beside the iron gate,
faint hunger in his eyes and twitching shame
in his hands, lips mumbling old stories
known as lies. Pressing against a car,
glancing at the men swarming from the mill
with swinging dinnerpails and a walk
much too stiff for buoyancy, not an eye
that sees him but grows hard and cold,
not a lip but tenses into a sneer,
not a hand but twists into an iron vise.
He stands there monument to our shame,
ugly echo of the day we lost our fear
and felt it fall from us a heavy weight
and strike! felt the power in our hands
thrust toward the ceiling in a chorus of ayes,
yes, by god, strike! and saw eyes shining with
remembered purpose, knew again
the proud magic of a clenched first. He led us,
his words were the mirror to our hopes.
Day after day, the net of his phrases
spun craftily, unbeautifully encompassing,
water drenching a clear flame to cold ashes.
Then one day, a conference held secretly,
the nodding of heads, the scratch of a pen,
and cigars chewed quite powerfully
by sleek sullen jaws. And we went back,
knowing again the old story forgotten,
some with feet leaden and the spirit dark,
some thrusting a finger into every wound,
and some braver for defeat, pain and hate
generating visions of a new dawn. While he,

he stayed outside. Alien eternally to our dreams,
our suffering, and our hope, to die at last,
potbellied and alone, brother only to contempt.

II

PAPERMILL

Not to be believed, this blunt savage wind
Blowing in chill empty rooms, this tornado
Surging and bellying across the oily floor
Pushing men out in streams before it;
Not to be believed, this dry fall
Of unseen fog drying the oil
And emptying the jiggling greasecups;
Not to be believed, this unseen hand
Weaving a filmy rust of spiderwebs
Over these turbines and grinding gears,
These snarling chippers and pounding jordans;
These fingers placed to lips saying shshsh:
Keep silent, keep silent, keep silent;
Not to be believed hardly, this clammy silence
Where once feet stamped over the oily floor,
Dinnerpails clattered, voices rose and fell
In laughter, curses, and songs. Now the guts
Of this mill have ceased and red changes to black,
Steam is cold water, silence is rust, and quiet
Spells hunger. Look at these men, now,
Standing before the iron gates, mumbling,
"Who could believe it? Who could believe it?"

PROSPERITY BLUES: MINNESOTA

It was good to watch the fatboys toedance like chorusgirls, warbling arias to prosperity, chanting, "We are the greatest nation that ever was," while the belly of capitalism swelled like a balloon until it touched the table—

sleep crept stealthily up our thighs flooding our brains with bromides and we forgot—

now the planingmill limps through the days, no orders no orders chant the timeclocks no orders come back tomorrow or the day after or next year, maybe—

yesterday or the day before or last year it was fun, maybe, to get a vacation, to go home and sit before the fire reading the newspapers telling how prosperous we were—

one isn't so bad, but another and another: well there's the kids at home, there's the house, there's the rent—

it's goodbye now to the secondhand Ford; it's howdoyoudo to the bill collector; it's goodbye now to the radio, to the new furniture; it's goodbye now to the bankbook—

now it isn't so funny anymore and it's queer, isn't it, how hymns to prosperity remind you of bullfrogs sitting on lilypads snapping at flies and croaking at the yellow moon?—

America is a fatman gorged with too much food, dying of indigestion. Too much prosperity, like too much meat, is bad for the stomach, and now America is slowly dying of auto-intoxication—

or the papermill . . . no more orders . . . down for ten days or twenty days or a month . . . and papermakers, aristocrats to their fingertips, now remember something as they get a job as sweepers in a sawmill saying goodbye to eight bucks a day, howdoyoudo three bucks—

no more orders no more orders is a tune to dance to, the New American Jazz; it is a tune that sweeps into the papermill like a great broom sweeping out workers; comes like a cold wind into the planingmill; howls like a gaunt hungry wolf down the canyons of lumber in the yard—

no orders, no orders, boys, nothing to do now but go home not smiling anymore—

remembering how sleep crept stealthily up our thighs flooding our minds with bromides and how we forgot!

THUNDER IN A MOMENT OF CALM

O lightning! slice the sky
with sudden amazing grins of flame.
O thunder! shout hoarsely from the sky
your deep black-throated challenge
to all small fragile trembling things.
O thunder! beat upon us,
have no pity for us,
who stand idly in the street
with dust in our eyes
awaiting rain
talking softly now or smirking
over nothing and nothing,
fumbling secretly for the wounds
of the week's unbeautiful toil
(bitterly sterile)
while there before us
the warm friendly earth
smiles and beckons and commands:
Comrades, take me, I am yours.
O thunder! chastise us
that for one instant
we should be humble
before these foul derbied men
flipping frayed cigars
into the street
from autos passing.
Enter into us hugely.
Give us of your roar
that we may have speech
for what we really mean to say.
Teach us your mad splendid fury.
Bring to us tokens of the storm

that shall bring the long-awaited rain
to ease the parched aching throats
of men standing sullenly in the streets.

UNEMPLOYED ANTHOLOGY

I

I stand on a streetcorner staring at a cigarette glowing between my fingers, my mind nibbling on an idea much as the small teeth of mice nibble a piece of cheese. It is this: I have saved so much money, and with careful attention, it will last me so many months. I compute carefully. I have so many brothers, a sister, and a mother. They must eat and I have no job. The windows of the sawmill are dull grey sheets; the tall black smokestacks haven't belched smoke for many days. The papermill lounges vacantly by the river, a brick mortuary of dead hours and minutes and timeclocks. The streets are dotted with forlorn men from whose faces much laughter has flown. Bitterness and fear walk arm in arm with men. What shall we do? What is the world coming to? Today we still have food. But what of tomorrow?

II.

He is an old man who was the first to go when they began to lay off men. He worked for the same company for fifteen years and in all that time he hasn't lost over six months. Now he is without work and spends his time rubbing shoulders with strong husky young men who pound the sidewalks with him, looking for work. He knows he will not find it. An old man has but a poor chance when there are hundreds of young men hungry and eager for jobs, who will take anything, who will do anything. Now he walks around the streets, or lies in the grass blinking at the sun, or goes to the dock and sits on a bench staring at the oily dark river flowing toward the dam that needs so little water these lean days. It is practically his first vacation, his first chance to blink at the sun and feel the kindly warmth of it steal up his thighs. He isn't happy. A dull perplexed look films his eyes and his forehead is puckered with worry. "I see by the papers," he says, "that there ain't going to be many old people left anymore. What do you think? Think there's going to be many old people living this year?"

III.

I met him in a poolhall sitting with the rest of the boys on the mourner's bench. He was well oiled and couldn't stand anymore. His face was that of one who drinks excessively. He red hair was tousled and his face was dirty. I sat beside him and said, "Jesus, but times are tough!" "Tough?" he looked at me and laughed. "Hell, times ain't tough. Why just last month I had a swell offer from the Heinz people, but I turned it down because I expect a better offer any time now. Sure, they offered me a job on the drive." "Drive?" I asked. "Hell, the Heinz people ain't in no lumbering business. They make pickles and catsup and rice flakes. What do you mean, drive?" "Didn't you hear about the drive?" he asked. "Where've you been? They offered me a job driving pickles down the Vinegar River, that's what they did." He laughed and I laughed with him, for it was funny. But he's just a type. Someday we'll hitch up our pants, spit on our hands, and dig into the big job of cleaning this fine land of ours of all its fat lice and bedbugs. But drunkards won't do it.

IV.

Another type: a machinist with a steady job. Naturally, he isn't worried, but since all the people talk about hard times, he has been infected too and has his own theories. He is one of those jackasses who can see no further than his nose and convinced that hard times depend on whether or not a Democrat or Republican is in office. "Let me tell you," he says, "the people are waking up. They won't stand it much longer. I bet you any money that our next president will be a Democrat. The people are fed up with Hoover. I bet good old Al Smith is laughing up his sleeve right now." Well, I thought, let "good old Al Smith" laugh up his sleeve if he wants to. Or if he wants to, he can cry. That won't buy me a job. That won't take the fear out of the hearts of men, or put laughter back into eyes grown dull, or bring back smiles to lips pressed together in a thin line of worry.

V.

Hendrickson was a lumberjack, and he was broke. I am sure of that because he borrowed a dollar from a friend to pay for his room. But that came out later. The fact is that times are tough for lumberjacks, with most of the camps down, and only gypos being hired. Hendrickson borrowed the dollar and rented a room in a hotel patronized by lumberjacks. What went through his mind then, I don't know, of course, but I have a hunch which I am keeping to myself. He stood before a mirror, looking at himself, probably grinning a bit. In his hand he held a razor. With a quick motion of his hand he cut his throat from ear to ear. After that it appears he continued to look at himself, bleeding. He walked around the room two or three times and finally toppled on the bed. These details, of course, are assumed, but the mute evidence consisting in trails of blood leading from the mirror around the room, speaks well for the soundness of the assumption. The next morning the landlord, coming to the room to tidy it up and open the window, found Hendrickson. The newspapers, of course, called it a "rash" act, which maybe it was. Further, they tell everybody interested enough, Hendrickson will be buried at the county's expense, he having no relatives and no money. One way to settle the unemployment problem!

VI.

He thinks of war and his face lights up. To him war is a magic ointment to be applied to the ailing rheumatic body of capitalism. "What we need," he says, "is another war. Then we'd have good times." The poor fish! He is twenty-eight years old, in sound physical condition, and would be one of the first to be drafted.

VII.

Revolution, "war between the rich class and the poor class," is an idea that sprouts like corn in fertile freshly plowed soil. The idea is immature, confused, bewildered, bungling, but still it is an idea. Men talk of it as thought it were inevitable. The talk is low and the intensity with which it is spoken varies. Some of the men talk viciously and blasphemously. Others quietly. Still others speak of it as though they were bystanders or members of an audience watching a tragedy. But we all talk. We all pound our heels on the pavements and keep shuffling around feeling the fear perched like a crow in our hearts, pecking at our minds, nibbling away our happiness and pride bit by bit, much like the small teeth of a mouse nibbling on a piece of cheese.

WORKER UPROOTED

The slow sleepy curl of cigarette smoke and butts
glowing redly out of moving smiling mouths;
now a whisper in the house, laughter muted,
and warm words spoken no more to me.
Alien, I move forlorn among curses,
laughing falsely, joking with tears
aching at my eyes, now surely alien and lonely.
Once I rubbed shoulders with sweating men,
pulled when they pulled, strained, cursed,
comrade in their laughter,
comrade in their pain,
knowing fellowship of sudden smiles
and the press of hands in silent speech.
At noon hour, sprawled in the shade,
opening our lunches, chewing our sandwiches,
laughing and spitting,
we talked of the days and found joy
in our anger, balm in our common contempt;
thought of lumber falling with thump of lead
on piles geometrically exact; of horses
sweating, puffing, bulging their muscles;
of wagons creaking; of sawdust
pouring from the guts of the mill.
Now alien, I move forlorn, an uprooted tree,
feel the pain of hostile eyes
lighting up no more for me;
the forced silence, the awkward laugh,
comrade no more in laughter and pain.

And at dawn, irresolutely,
into the void . . .

ARCHITECT

An old beggar, bleary-eyed with hope forlorn,
sat by a roadside
banking with sandy sides a drunken ditch,
and wept his rusty tears into the slimy stream.
His head was light with whiskey,
his feet refused him guidance
and his soggy heart
was sore.

A tramp he was,
filthy, lousy with bugs that hid
with needled feet in his hairy hide . . .
an awful stench of sweaty underclothes . . .
and wounded shoes baring dirty toes . . .

Hands . . .
red, grimy, and fat,
well versed in laziness and sin.

The tramp, the old beggar
wept.
With shaky nervous hands he built
a castle out of the clay
that banked the ditch.
It rose majestic, and in his vacant mind
where such thoughts had long since
swam their way to oblivion in glistening streams
of wine, beer, and brandy,
it seemed a happy home,
with wife and children
to adore him . . .

He staggered upright.
Clenching his fat hands he looked to God
and swore.

"I'm going back. I'm through with this dirty bumming.
God I have found you.
I will adore you.
I will never leave you again."

The tramp, the old beggar,
being rather unsteady on his wobbly legs
lost his balance
and fell with a resounding thud
on his hand-built castle
crunching his dream
into gaudy spurts of clay.

He grinned.
Rather unsteadily he got to his feet,
and slowly,
with a lagging tear resting on his cheek,
he staggered off,
to find drink,
to find women . . .

Old tramp, old beggar,
do you know what dreams are now?

POOLROOM FACES

Faces floating in a poolroom fog,
faces flowering out of collars
and shirts like greenhouse cabbages,
faces with eyes tired, eyes like pools
filmed over with fog, sad and vacant eyes
like bright coals burned to grey cinders.
Men sitting on poolroom chairs
staring at the floor with vacant eyes
blinking as the last billiard ball
rolls smooth as hell into the right pocket;
seeing and not seeing, seeing phlegm
glistening like jewels in the yellow light,
smoldering cigarette butts, gum wrappers,
cigarette packages; hearing sharp sudden click
of billiard balls, low loving entreaties
of players finding life concentrated in a cue.
Faces, now so unlovely and sad,
were you ever wise and resolute? O corpse faces,
pasty faces, dead faces, did your eyes
ever smolder with creative hate?

Faces growing on that evil sour apple tree,
withered fruit of sour poisoned stalk,
sad harvest of work and looking for work,
harvest of mine, harvest of factory,
harvest of lumbercamp and sectiongang,
poolroom faces gazing at poolroom floor,
waiting, thinking maybe, wishing a little,
praying for strong men to plow the sour soil!

UNEMPLOYED

In the shadow of a poolhall he stands limply. It will soon be night. Twilight now is a soft fall of grey ashes. Look: twilight is a dry fog settling on brothels, falling on blindpigs, falling on poolhalls, cigarstores, cafes. It will soon be night. Darkness creeps stealthily over the papermill, blotting piles of broken lumber, blotting boxcars, piles of sulfite screenings, blotting junkpile, ashpile, coalpile. It will soon be night. Nothing now but dull glow of windows. He looks, his body sagging limply. A cigarette glows between his fingers. He is quite alone. It is a very cold night. The people he wants to see and watch as they walk down the sidewalk are still at home eating supper. He doubts if they will come tonight. It is a very cold night and it looks like rain. The clouds have whispered it, the wind telegraphs, the smoke promises. From the papermill a vile jetting of sulfur dioxide. It settles in a stinking fog. It burns in the nostrils, penetrates, sweeps down alleys, settles on vacant lots, fills the street. Now distantly there is a throb, a muffled overture of wheels, pulleys, beaters, grinders, and escaping steam. The nightshift is at work. He is not working.

It had been done quite simply. He remembered walking over the slippery greasy floor, a thin film gliding over his eyes and a quiet calm flowing to his lips; he remembered how tired his legs were from pressing down levers and how they trembled in relaxation; he remembered words walking coldly on thin lips; remembered a small white discharge slip, his laughter by the gate, his sudden fierce anger, his clenched fist.

It was done always so simply. Words walking through thinfat lips and there tomorrow a man stands on streetcorners futile cold and hungry fingers of his loneliness reaching out to touch people hurrying by him with an icy stare, a dry fog settling down upon him O suddenly most surely a little brown dog wagging his tail asking for handpats aching with hunger wincing at thoughts of tomorrows endlessly on parade.

Or Chicago. Waves smashing into splinters of green on the lakefront a cold breeze dancing over the lake the zoom of traffic roar of the elevated beating upon him sitting on a parkbench watching lovers disappear into shrubbery and he sitting there looking stupidly numb with cold. God. Or walking, for instance, over Clark Street Bridge odor of roasted coffee not quite overwhelming odor of garbage pulled by puffing tugs, and a policeman dogging his steps. Or West Madison Street smell of sour sweat thick on the air and canned heat and a man sidling to him touching his shoulder come with me dearie I will give you something to eat. God. Or watching the sharkboards hoping and not hoping wishing and not wishing wanting and not wanting, apathy and fear steaming up his legs, depressing his heart, and God how he did want to cry.

Or Cincinnati. And a small jew eyeing him coldly sneering, his eyes walking over frayed edges of his overcoat frayed trousers wrinkled tie walking coldly over his face and hair cut not quite in the latest fashion and God how his soul whimpered and snuffled and crept into the dark kennels of despair to turn crouching hate flowering darkly within him hands longing to grasp the sleek throat throttling until sharkboards wantads breadlines flopjoints crumbled into dust and were one with the dark earth and beauty flowered over all the land.

Or sitting there anywhere now or then or tomorrow slowly a contraction of his Being more and more insignificant until he was a flea or a paintpimple on a parkbench or a cockroach crawling repulsively over the pavement and the beautiful girls their legs always walking away and drawing away and he so wanting a white hand running gently through his hair.

Or Minneapolis. Omaha. Detroit. Cleveland. Seattle. Always boxcars rattling over gleaming rails always parallel the earth always feeling and responding always: the dark cool maternal earth. Always a magnet always calling always crying to him to speed away from his pain futile and hungry and he wanting to smash things and a cold clean wind from the east beating upon him pushing him pushing him pushing pushing right through him beyond him beyond civilization and policemen and scabs and hunger and words walking through thinfat lips beyond a tomorrow that is but the crack of a pistol beginning the march of tomorrows and tomorrows endlessly on parade.

Christ, he mutters, suddenly, his fingers grasping a cigarette he has forgotten to puff. He flips the butt into the street, leaves shadows of the poolhall, and walks quickly away, his legs trembling a bit in relaxation.

NOW THAT SNOW IS FALLING

O the sky shall crack with laughter
now that snow is falling,
and all small timid things shall scent
frozen petals of white and feel
knifeblades of cold sink into fur;
yes, the bear shall suck his toes,
and ants will sleep.
If the sun, coming slowly after,
warms flies from frozen lethargy
to crawl again upon window panes,
and you and I, hand in hand,
shall make tracks in the snow,
woolen gloves, and necks bound warmly
against knifeblades of cold, and we
shall say: O most surely is the snow
beautiful, and ask, what can we say
now that snow is falling, and all
the world is white, and clean, and beautiful,
what can we say but that snow is beautiful
and snow tingles the sleepy blood
into new surging awareness—what can
we say if the sky is most suddenly rent
with laughter, trees crack with mirth,
and sparrows chatter in derision, as
a man walks by us clad thinly, shivering,
hungry, vainly searching for bread,
a job, and warm fires; what can we say,
if such a man passes us bowed against
the wind, and another, and yet more,
until he is as a multitude, a sad parade
of hungry, cold, vague faces? What can we
say, now that snow is falling?

BANK

Be proud whimpers
the bank be proud with
compound interest and
mortgages on farms lean
and not so lean . . .
O blueprint under eyes
manifestly curves pillars
burglaralarms O eyes
warm with wine of massive
granite . . .
Addingmachines, ledgers,
president with black cigar,
and bookkeeper scanning
stockexchange reports have
a beauty too . . .
Be proud be proud workmen
glance at surplus fund
deposits receipts with eyes
warm as eyes gliding over
what must not be said . . .
Be proud be proud whimpers
the bank be proud to a bum
with crooked legs and cinders
in his eyes be proud to a bum
diffidently picking at his nose
and with blunt nails,
scratching at his ear.

FLAGWAVER

When I get patriotic, I go on a big drunk.
Let me tell you—
patriotism is a shot of snow, a whiff of opium,
a mouthful of rotgut strong enough
to eat the brass pants off a monkey.
Let me tell you—
when the flag waves in redwhiteblue frenzy,
when fat men stand on platforms with thumbs hooked
Napoleon-wise in lapels of their coats
expounding landoffreemen,
telling me America is my sweetheart,
I get patriotic as hell,
I go on the big drunk.

When I get patriotic, I go on the big drunk.
I cut Wesley Everest, I hang that black Injun
Frank Little from a bridge, I put Joe Hill
against a wall and fill the lousy bastard
with hot jets of lead,
I break the foreign heads of strikers,
them yella slackers, them chickenlivered
bastards.

When I get patriotic, I go on a spree.
I go on the big drunk.

TO THE MURDERERS OF HARRY SIMMS

I.

Harry Simms. Communist. 19 years old. Murdered.
Harry Simms. Dreamer. Fighter. Boy.
We'll make a poster about that.
We'll hang it up on the walls of your rotten
rat-devoured world.
We'll hang it up where the rust of dark dead days
will never gnaw the least small word.
We'll hang it up where we can always see,
so that the thought of you and you and you,
will always be a retching in the foul gutters
of your decaying world.

II.

Surely today now the frog mouths of you are smiling.
Surely surely you are today spitting the foul phlegm
of your minds in the unwashed spittoons
of your world.
Surely surely the hog jaws of you are slavering today:
"We got him, we got the bastard, we got the Red.
It was rich, wasn't it, the way the hospital
wouldn't let him in for an hour
until the bill was made good,
and him lying there, bleeding at the guts?"

Surely today now your world of bills, hunger, and death,
looks very good to you,
doesn't it, gentlemen?

III.

And if the sun shines
licking the wounds of our toil with warm soft tongue,
and if the clouds sail gracefully before it,
and the stars shine,
and grasses soft under foot
remind us that the world is good

and life is very beautiful,
still we shall remember
the cancer of capitalism gnawing at the heart
of this, our warm beautiful world.

And the softness of the days shall not rust
the steel of our hearts
nor the iron of our purpose!

INVOCATION TO THE WIND

O sprinting of the wind over land
like a colt galloping swift
pounding over grass, neighing
to the sun, snorting howdoyoudo
to the clouds, with a flying mane—
O wind coming over the lean land
like a fatness of green in spring
or flowers blooming in Mojave
blow, blow into all dusty corners,
reach cool fingers beyond cobwebs
festooning this dark room where
throats are choked with dust and
beauty shrivels like mushrooms
in dry cellars—blow, blow, blow
into factories with windows of dust
and a shuffling of feet tired
in silk stockings, and fingers
red at the tips—blow, blow into
jail, come like a draught of spring
water to faces hungering against
steel bars—blow, blow into slums,
cleave the darkness festering
in mines, coal and iron, glide over
pale children bowing in beetfields—
blow wind, spring over the land
like a colt pounding over grass—
rattle the shutters of this dark room
where beauty whimpers softly like a child—
O surely someday we'll fill the fields
with our dancing and laughing and singing,
O wind coming over the lean brown land
or flowers creeping over Mojave!

RESIGNATION

Let there be no weeping, friends,
when I return to the ground,
just the sound of church bells calling
and the thud of hard clods falling
on my wooden box, scented and sound.
Let there be no weeping, friends.

Sources

"Night-Shift" published in *International Literature* (March 1934).

"Proletarian Night" published in *International Literature* (November 1934).

"The Way It Goes" published in *The Spider* 1, no. 5 (May 1928).

"Dust of Iron Ore" published in *The Left* 1, no. 1 (Spring 1931); and under the title "Episodes Traced in Iron Ore" in *New Masses* (May 1931).

"Funeral" published in the *Daily Worker* (date unknown); and reprinted in *Unrest: Rebel Poets' Anthology for 1929.*

"Warm Day in Papermill Town" published in *The Left* 1, no. 2 (Autumn 1931).

"Greenlumber Chain" publication information unknown.

"Sawdust" published in *The Whirl* (date unknown).

"A Gypo in Sawdust" published in *New Masses* (August 1929).

"Testament" unpublished; circa 1927.

"They Blow Whistles for the New Year" published in *New Masses* (January 1929); and reprinted in *Unrest: Rebel Poets' Anthology for 1929.*

"Mesaba Impressions" published in *The New Magazine* (March 1927).

"Repentant Judas" published in *New Masses* (July 1934).

"Papermill" published in *Front* (April 1931); and reprinted in *Unrest: Rebel Poets' Anthology for 1931.*

"Prosperity Blues" published in *New Masses* (March 1930).

"Thunder in a Moment of Calm" published in *The Anvil* (May-June 1935).

"Unemployed Anthology" published in *New Masses* (September 1930).

"Worker Uprooted" published in *New Masses* (February 1932).

"Architect" unpublished; circa 1928.

"Poolroom Faces" published in *New Masses* (December 1931); and reprinted in *The Rebel Poet* (1931).

"Unemployed" published in *The Morada* 2 (1929).

"Now that Snow is Falling" published in *New Masses* (January 1930); and reprinted in *Unrest: Rebel Poets' Anthology for 1930.*

"Bank" published in *The Morada* 2 (1929).

"Flagwaver" published in *New Masses* (October 1928).

"To the Murderers of Harry Simms" published in *International Literature* 3 (July 1933).

"Invocation to the Wind" published in *The Morada* 3 (1930); and reprinted in *Unrest: Rebel Poets' Anthology for 1930.*

"Resignation" unpublished; circa 1927.

TED GENOWAYS is author of *Bullroarer: A Sequence* and editor of several books, including *Hard Time: Life in a State Prison, 1849–1914*, *The Selected Poems of Miguel Hernández*, and *A Perfect Picture of Hell: Eyewitness Accounts by Civil War Prisoners from the 12th Iowa*. His poems have earned numerous awards, including the Natalie Ornish Poetry Award, the Pushcart Prize, a 2003 NEA Fellowship in Poetry, and two Guy Owen Poetry Prizes from *Southern Poetry Review*. He is currently editor of the *Virginia Quarterly Review*.

The American Poetry Recovery Series

Collected Poems   *Edwin Rolfe; edited by Cary Nelson and Jefferson Hendricks*
Trees Became Torches: Selected Poems   *Edwin Rolfe; edited by Cary Nelson and Jefferson Hendricks*
Palace-Burner: The Selected Poetry of Sarah Piatt   *Edited and with an introduction by Paula Bernat Bennett*
Black Moods: Collected Poems   *Frank Marshall Davis; edited by John Edgar Tidwell*
Rendezvous with Death: American Poems of the Great War   *Edited by Mark W. Van Wienen*
The Wound and the Dream: Sixty Years of American Poems about the Spanish Civil War   *Edited by Cary Nelson*
Collected Poems   *Don Gordon; edited and with an essay by Fred Whitehead*
Complete Poems   *Claude McKay; edited and with an introduction by William J. Maxwell*
The Whole Song: Selected Poems   *Vincent Ferrini; edited and with an introduction by Kenneth A. Warren and Fred Whitehead*
Wicked Times: Selected Poems   *Aaron Kramer; edited and with a biographical essay by Cary Nelson and Donald Gilzinger Jr.*
Papermill   *Joseph Kalar; edited and with an introduction by Ted Genoways*

The University of Illinois Press
is a founding member of the
Association of American University Presses.

Composed in 10/13.5 Berkeley Oldstyle
with Helvetica Neue and Fell Type Roman display
by Jim Proefrock
at the University of Illinois Press
Designed by Paula Newcomb
Manufactured by Thomson-Shore, Inc.

University of Illinois Press
1325 South Oak Street
Champaign, IL 61820-6903
www.press.uillinois.edu